The Telephone

Illustrated by Jean-Marie Poissenot
Created by Gallimard Jeunesse
and Claude Delafosse

MOONLIGHT PUBLISHING / FIRST DISCOVERY

The telephone is an amazing invention!
People can speak to one another
all around the world.

In most cities, you can phone from a public booth in the street.

Telephones have changed over the years. Now they are often brightly coloured, with push buttons instead of dials.

But how did we communicate before telephones?

In Ancient Greece, 2,500 years ago, a messenger ran 42 kilometres non-stop. He had to tell the king of victory against the Persians at Marathon.

He gave the news
to the king, but
died of exhaustion!

In ancient civilisations, a horn blast warned that the enemy was coming.

In Africa, a tom-tom carried news of births, feasts, deaths, coronations...

In Europe, the tabor drum made people stop and listen to an announcement.

Church bells rang out the hour, or called people to prayer.

Morse code uses dots and dashes to stand for letters of the alphabet. Messages were sent along a telegraph wire

Messages in Morse code
could also be sent as
a series of flashes of light.

This semaphore was used
to send signals by changing
the position of its arms.

Over the years,
people have found
many different ways
to send messages!

Carrier pigeons flew long distances
with a message wrapped around one leg.

Native Americans
used smoke signals...

... to let friends across the mountains know
that a wagon train of pioneers was on its way.

In the Middle Ages, monks carried
news as they travelled from
one monastery to another.

In the 19th century,
stage coaches carried mail
quickly across Britain.

Nowadays,
high speed trains
do the job even better!

In the American Wild West,
Pony Express riders
ran the first mail service.

Aeroplanes have carried
mail since 1911.

But it is the postman
who delivers letters
to your home each day.

When you have stamped
your letter, you can send
it almost anywhere
in the world.

Can you tell
which country each
postcard has been
sent from?

You can stay in one place
as your voice travels,
through walls, across cities
countries, and even continents!

The first telephone
were heavy an
they were fixe
in place

The telephone was
invented in 1876.

Now you can
carry a mobile phone
with you, and make calls
from anywhere.

This is
a fax machine.
You can send
text or pictures
drawn on paper.
Messages
travel down the
telephone line.

After a few seconds, perhaps on the other side of the world, paper comes out of another fax machine. The message looks just like your original!

Satellites in space beam telephone signals across oceans. They also receive and send

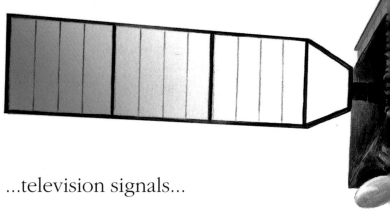

...television signals...

...radio signals...

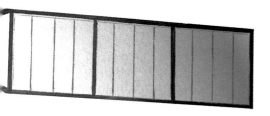

...and signals
for computer
systems.

Walkie-talkies can do the work of telephones
over short distances.

Lifeguard

Policeman

Foreman
on a building site

In certain jobs, you need a walkie-talkie.

But it's not just useful for work!
How do you think the boy
knows where the girl
is hiding with the picnic?

To make a telephone,
you need two yoghurt
pots and a ball of string.
Make a hole in the base
of each pot and stretch
the string tightly
between the two.

Like telegraphers in days gone by,
you can send messages in Morse code.
All you need is a torch.

. short flash
_ longer flash

A ._	J .___	S ...	1 .____
B _...	K _._	T _	2 ..___
C _._.	L ._..	U .._	3 ...__
D _..	M __	V ..._	4 ...._
E .	N _.	W .__	5 .....
F .._.	O ___	X _.._	6 _....
G __.	P .__.	Y _.__	7 __...
H	Q __._	Z __..	8 ___..
I ..	R ._.	É ..._..	9 ____.
			0 _____

FIRST DISCOVERY – pioneering the exciting technique
of the double-sided printed overlay. More titles are available:

ABOUT ANIMALS
THE EGG
BIRDS
THE OWL
THE EAGLE
PENGUINS
FARM ANIMALS
THE ELEPHANT
WHALES
THE HORSE
MONKEYS & APES
THE BEAVER
BEARS
CATS
THE WOLF
THE MOUSE
THE LADYBIRD
THE BEE
THE BUTTERFLY
THE FROG
DINOSAURS

ABOUT PEOPLE
COLOURS
COUNTING
UP & DOWN
TIME
LIGHT
PICTURES
SHAPES
MUSIC

PYRAMIDS
HOMES
THE BUILDING SITE
THE TOWN
THE CASTLE
CATHEDRALS
CLOTHES AND COSTUMES
AMERICAN INDIANS
FLYING
ON WHEELS
BOATS
TRAINS
SPORT
THE TOOLBOX
THE TELEPHONE
HANDS, FEET AND PAWS
BABIES
THE BODY

ABOUT NATURE
FLOWERS
FRUIT
VEGETABLES
THE TREE
WATER
THE RIVERBANK
UNDER THE GROUND
THE JUNGLE
EARTH AND SKY
THE SEASHORE
WEATHER

Translator: Clare Best
Editorial adviser: Sarah Angliss
ISBN 1 85103 237 1
© 1995 by Editions Gallimard
English text © 1996 by Moonlight Publishing Ltd
First published in the United Kingdom 1996
by Moonlight Publishing Ltd, 36 Stratford Road, London W8
Printed in Italy by Editoriale Libraria